LAOS

MAJOR WORLD NATIONS
LAOS

Ralph Zickgraf

CHELSEA HOUSE PUBLISHERS
Philadelphia

Chelsea House Publishers

Contributing Author: Margie Buckmaster

Copyright © 1999 by Chelsea House Publishers,
a division of Main Line Book Co.
Printed and bound in the United States of America.

First Printing

1   3   5   7   9   8   6   4   2

Library of Congress Cataloging-in-Publication Data applied for

ISBN 0–7910–4743–1

CONTENTS

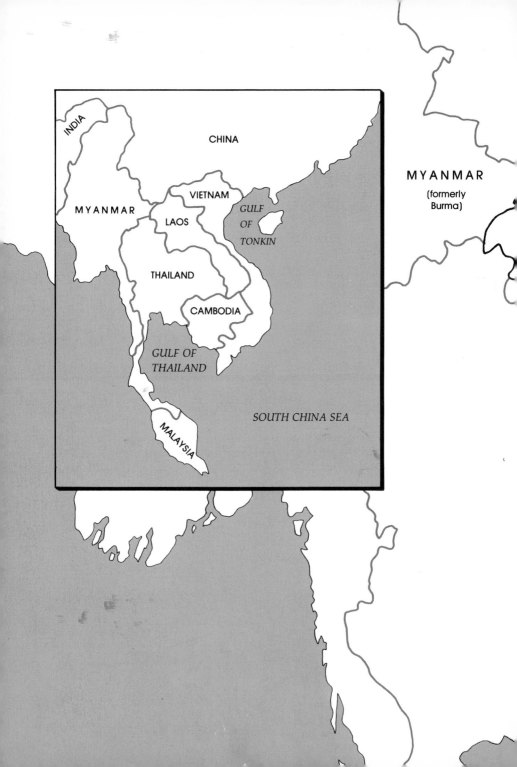

INDIA

CHINA

MYANMAR

VIETNAM

LAOS

GULF
OF
TONKIN

THAILAND

CAMBODIA

GULF OF
THAILAND

MALAYSIA

SOUTH CHINA SEA

MYANMAR
(formerly
Burma)

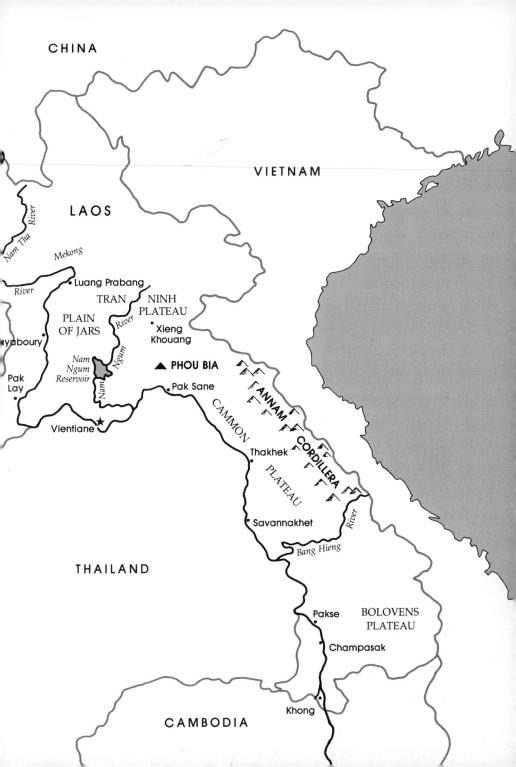

FACTS AT A GLANCE

Land and People

Official Name	Lao People's Democratic Republic
Area	91,430 square miles (236,800 square kilometers)
Capital	Vientiane (population 377,000)
Terrain	Rugged and mountainous
Highest Point	Phou Bia, 9,250 feet (2,820 meters)
Major Rivers	Mekong, Nam Ngum, Bang Fai
Natural Resources	Tin, timber, hydroelectric power
Climate	Tropical, with a rainy monsoon season lasting from May to October
Population	4,975,000
Population Density	48 people per square mile (18.6 per square kilometer)
Population Distribution	81 percent rural; 19 percent urban
Birth Rate	42 per 1,000 population
Infant Mortality Rate	97 per 1,000 live births

Average Life Expectancy	Male, 51 years; female, 51 years
Official Language	Lao
Other Languages	French, English
Religions	Buddhism, 85 percent; tribal, 15 percent
Ethnic Groups	Laos is populated by 68 tribes and ethnic minorities classified into 4 major ethnic groups: the Lao Lum and Lao Tai, counted together by the government (68 percent); the Lao Theung (22 percent); and the Lao Soung (9 percent)

Economy

Currency	*kip*, divided into 100 *at*
Major Trading Partners	Thailand, Vietnam, Japan
Major Exports	Hydroelectric power, timber, tin
Major Imports	Machinery, petroleum products, foodstuffs
Chief Agricultural Products	Rice, corn, tobacco, fruit, vegetables

Government

Form of Government	Single-party people's republic
Chief of State	President
Head of Government	Prime minister

HISTORY AT A GLANCE

1353–73 Fa Ngum unifies scattered principalities into the kingdom of Lan Xang. Theravada Buddhism becomes the state religion.

1373 Fa Ngum is deposed by his son, Sam Sene Thai, who rules until 1416.

1478 Annam invades Lan Xang and captures the royal capital.

1479 King Thene Kham (1479–86) drives the Annamese out of Lan Xang.

1547 King Photisarath (1520–47) seizes the throne of neighboring Chiengmai and installs his son Sethathirath as its king. Sethathirath succeeds his father as king of Lan Xang. He returns to the capital of Lan Xang with the Emerald Buddha (Pra Keo). He repels two Burmese invasions but loses the kingdom of Chiengmai to the Burmese and moves the royal capital to Vientiane.

1571 Sethathirath disappears while on an expedition against rebellious hill tribes and is succeeded by his son Sened Soulintha (1571–82).

1574   Lan Xang is overrun by Burmese armies.

1591   Lan Xang regains its independence from Burma.

1637   Souligna Vongsa gains the throne after a struggle among competing factions of the royal family. His reign (1637–94) is considered the Golden Age of Lan Xang.

1641   Dutch merchant Gerrit van Wuysthoff is the first recorded European to visit present-day Laos.

1700   With help from Annam, a nephew of Souligna Vongsa seizes the throne from his grandson, Kitsarath. The conflict between factions causes the breakup of the kingdom of Lan Xang.

1707   Kitsarath sets up rule in the north, establishing the principality of Luang Prabang.

1713   The southern part of Lan Xang breaks away and becomes the principality of Champasak. The remaining central part of Lan Xang becomes the principality of Vientiane.

1752   Burma conquers Luang Prabang.

1778   Siam drives the Burmese out of Luang Prabang and conquers Vientiane.

1802   Vientiane expels the Siamese but comes under control of Annam.

1826   Prince Anou of Vientiane invades Siam but is driven back.

1829   Siam conquers Vientiane, burns the capital, and carries the Pra Keo back to Bangkok.

1886   Auguste Pavie is appointed French vice-consul to Luang Prabang.

1887   Luang Prabang becomes a French protectorate.

1893   Siam gives up all claim to Vientiane and Luang Prabang, which together become the French Protectorate of Laos.

1894–1907 Treaties with Siam and Burma establish new borders for Laos, mostly defined by the course of the Mekong River.

1940 Japan occupies the Indochina peninsula but leaves the French colonial administration intact.

1941 Japan forces Laos to cede land on the right bank of the Mekong to Siam and establishes the king of Luang Prabang as ruler of all Laos.

1945 The Japanese force King Sisavang Vong (1904–59) to declare Laos independent of France, but after Japan's surrender the French reoccupy Laos.

1945–54 The First Indochina War. Nationalist rebels in Laos, Vietnam, and Cambodia fight to oust the French.

1949 Laos becomes an independent state within the French Union.

1954 In the Geneva Peace Agreement, Laos is declared a fully independent, neutral nation. Vietnam is divided into two countries, North and South Vietnam.

1955–75 The Second Indochina War. Communist rebels in Laos fight to overthrow the royal government. The United States bombs North Vietnamese supply lines in Laos, and the U.S. Central Intelligence Agency (CIA) bankrolls and conducts a "secret war" in Laos.

1961 The Geneva Peace Congress reconvenes and reaffirms Laotian neutrality. The secret war continues, however. Laos is divided; Communist forces control the northeastern and eastern half of the country while the royal government fights to retain control of the rest.

1975 After the United States pulls out of the war, South Vietnam falls, and rebels seize control in Laos and Cambodia. King Savang Vatthana of

Laos resigns, and the Pathet Lao proclaims the establishment of the Lao People's Democratic Republic.

1977 Laos signs a 25-year treaty of friendship with Vietnam.

1980s Laos works to develop its education and public health systems.

1987 The government announces the New Economic Management System, a program to improve the nation's struggling economy.

1989 Laos holds its first nationwide election since 1975 and opens its doors to Western tourists for the first time since the 1950s.

1990s Laos abandons economic communism for capitalism, but the single-party regime retains tight political control.

LAOS

Smoke rises from the *Plain of Jars* after a Royal Lao Air Force bombing raid in May 1964. The territory was under the control of the Pathet Lao, a Communist-backed rebel group that eventually prevailed in Laos's long civil war. Throughout its history, Laos has often been vexed by internal conflicts and foreign wars. It has also served as the battleground for fighting between its larger, more powerful neighbors.

1

Laos and the World

Laos is a land in the middle. It lies in the center of the Indochina peninsula, in the rugged country between the Mekong River and the chain of mountains called the Annam Cordillera. The people of Laos are a mixture of ethnic and tribal groups shaped by the intersection of two expanding civilizations, India and China. As the centerpiece of a geopolitical jigsaw puzzle, Laos has often been the battleground for conflicts with and between its larger and more powerful neighbors.

Colonization by France in the late 19th century brought temporary peace. To the French, Laos was a dreamy landscape of jungle-shrouded mountains and misty river valleys, inhabited by gentle, graceful people whose cultural identity had survived centuries of invasion and political domination by Annam (now Vietnam), Siam (now Thailand), and Burma (now Myanmar).

After World War II, Laos was once again caught between opposing forces, this time worldwide. During the war, Japan had ousted France from its colonial possessions (which included Laos) on the Indochina peninsula. Following Japan's surrender in 1945, France reclaimed its colonies but agreed to grant limited autonomy to Laos,

Vietnam, and Cambodia. Movements for national independence grew within each country, however, and people sought to free their lands from French control. Eventually, all of Southeast Asia was swept by strong nationalist movements as its peoples demanded the freedom to choose their own government. This regional struggle for self-determination soon became part of a larger conflict between world superpowers. The United States supported France, and the Soviet Union and China supported the rebel groups, many of which were led by Communists. Following a devastating military defeat at Dien Bien Phu, Vietnam, in 1954, France withdrew from the region. The United States continued to back anti-Communist governments, and the Soviet Union and China continued to support leftist liberation movements.

Nationalism and the struggle for independence on the Indochina peninsula led to a struggle between two political systems, capitalism and communism. Laos was once again caught in the middle. As in neighboring Vietnam, the United States and the Soviet Union vented their mutual hostility by supporting warring factions in Laos. Thus, the 20th century came to Laos—a land of Buddhist monks, water buffalo, and dragon fireworks—in the form of screaming jets, helicopters, and destructive bombs. Unable to secure a military victory, U.S. troops finally left the peninsula in 1975. After the fall of South Vietnam and Cambodia to Communist contingents, the Pathet Lao, a Communist group that formed part of Laos's coalition government, assumed full control of the country in December 1975 and established the Lao People's Democratic Republic.

The triumph of Communist forces in Laos, Vietnam, and Cambodia did not, however, bring an end to political and military conflict. Boundary disputes and other disagreements between Vietnam and the brutal regime of the dictator Pol Pot in Kampuchea (as Cambodia was then called) led to a Vietnamese invasion of Kampuchea in December 1978. Vietnamese troops overthrew the

A gateway with posters, which urge the people to help build a socialist nation in Laos, frames That Luang, an ancient Buddhist shrine in the capital city of Vientiane.

government of Pol Pot and installed a puppet government under Heng Samrin. However, Vietnam's invasion of Kampuchea led to a break with China, which attacked Vietnam in early 1979.

Tensions have eased considerably since then. Bowing to international pressure, Vietnam withdrew its troops from Cambodia in 1989, and the United Nations helped rebuild an independent Cambodian government. But political turmoil still simmers in the region. Laos, as always, remains in the middle.

Vientiane, the capital of Laos, stretches out along the banks of the Mekong. With a population of 442,000, Vientiane is the largest city in Laos.

2

The Land

East of India, below China, the continent of Asia bulges into the South China Sea to form the Indochina peninsula. The peninsula consists mainly of three parallel chains of steeply folded mountain ranges. These mountain chains, which are merely spurs of the mighty Himalayan system, run from northwest to southeast. Great rivers, such as the Irrawaddy and the Mekong, drain the highlands, and most of the people of the region live in the rivers' valleys and on their fertile floodplains. The easternmost mountain range on the Indochina peninsula is called the Annam Cordillera. Its peaks vary in height from 9,250 to 6,000 feet (2,800 to 1,800 meters). Laos lies along the western slopes of the range, which separates the nation from its eastern neighbor, Vietnam.

Laos is approximately 600 miles (1,000 kilometers) long and 330 miles (550 kilometers) wide in the northwest. The narrow southeastern panhandle is at places fewer than 100 miles (133 kilometers) wide. The total area of Laos is 91,430 square miles (236,800 square kilometers), about the size of the United Kingdom or the state of Wyoming.

Laos is landlocked; that is, it is surrounded by other countries and has no coastline. It is bordered on the east by Vietnam, on the south by Cambodia, on the west by Thailand, on the northwest by Myanmar, and on the north by China. Dense jungle and rugged mountains dominate the terrain, and deep, narrow valleys slice through the mountains, particularly in the rugged northwest. The valleys have been cut by streams that flow southeast to the Mekong River, which forms most of Laos's borders with Myanmar and Thailand.

Laos has few roads and no railroads, and air transportation is scarce and expensive. Along the Mekong and its tributaries, people move themselves and their goods by water in an amazing variety of vessels. Stately junks, powered by sails or diesel-driven propellers, ply the wide reaches of the lower river. Sampans, flat-bottomed barges with two to four sets of oars, work the harbors. In the narrow upper reaches of the Mekong and on its swift tributaries, pirogues (canoes) skim the water. Pirogues range from 10 to 30 feet (3 to 9 meters) in length and are powered by paddles or outboard motors.

In addition to serving as the country's principal highway, the Mekong is the center of economic activity in Laos. All of the major towns are on the Mekong, and the river is the primary source of life for the people who live along it. The Mekong deposits rich topsoil every year on its banks and floodplains, enabling Laotians to plant such crops as rice, wheat, and many varieties of vegetables. Fish from the river are a major source of protein.

Laos has a tropical monsoon climate, which means that it is a land simultaneously lush and nutrient poor. The year-round heat of the tropics supports rich vegetation but also stimulates the growth of bacteria, which deplete the soil of minerals and nutrients. This process is called laterization, and red laterite soil is common throughout the tropics. When the land is covered with jungle or monsoon forest, dying trees and shrubs return enough nutrients to the thin upper layer of soil to promote new growth. But when

In a quiet pool beside the Mekong, villagers fish from their wooden sampans. The Mekong is Laos's principal transportation artery and the center of the nation's economic activity.

farmers clear the land and plant crops, the soil's nutrients are exhausted after two or three harvests, which is what happens in the mountains where tribespeople practice swidden, or slash-and-burn, agriculture. They clear the land with fire and ax and plant their crops in the ashes. When the nutrients in the soil are depleted, the farmers move to another piece of forest or jungle and repeat the process. The abandoned fields grow back in scrub, or in imperata grass, whose head-high blades are sharp enough to slash clothing and skin.

The Monsoons

Monsoons, seasonal winds that sweep over Asia in cyclic streams, determine the pattern of life for millions of people. In summer, the Northern Hemisphere is heated by the sun, which warms the vast land mass of Asia. Cool, wet air from the ocean passes over the warm land and, in the process, drops its moisture in torrents of rain. This is the summer monsoon, and it is awaited and prayed for from the east coast of Africa to the plains of eastern China. The summer monsoon also brings rain to the Indochina peninsula.

In Laos, the rainy season lasts from May to October. Vientiane, the capital, receives an average 12 inches (30 centimeters) a month from May to October. The average temperature during that period is 80° Fahrenheit (27° Centigrade). During the dry season (November to April), less than 2 inches a month, on average, falls on Vientiane, and the average temperature falls to about 70° Fahrenheit (21° Centigrade).

Rainfall varies throughout Laos. In the northwest, the winds from the Indian Ocean lose much of their moisture in the mountains of Myanmar, and the city of Luang Prabang averages about 50 inches (127 centimeters) of rain annually. In contrast, the Bolovens Plateau in the southern panhandle receives on the average more than 100 inches (254 centimeters) of rain a year. The monsoon rains cause the annual flooding of the Mekong and its tributaries, which makes the life-sustaining wet-rice agriculture of Laos possible.

Through Laos Along the Mekong

The Mekong, which is 2,600 miles (4,200 kilometers) in length, is the longest river in Southeast Asia. From its sources in the highlands of Tibet, it flows 1,200 miles (2,000 kilometers) south through China's Yunnan Province before reaching Laos, where it takes a southwest course. For 125 miles (200 kilometers) the Mekong rushes through a narrow gorge between the rugged mountains along the Laos-Myanmar border. It then turns to the southeast, forming part of the border with Thailand. This area is the heart of the Golden Triangle, one of the major opium-producing areas in the world. The borders of three nations come together here, but no government holds sway over the inhabitants of this remote wilderness. They owe their allegiance to tribal chiefs, and power rests in the hands of the warlords of the various tribes.

Opium is the dried resin from the opium poppy. Each year, just before the rainy season, tribespeople clear remote jungle hillsides by fire and plant poppies in the ashes. After the plants have flowered, workers cut slits in the tightly packed seed pods. They then collect the resin that has oozed out and dried in the sun. Armed caravans carry the resin over the mountains to Bangkok, Thailand, or to Rangoon, Myanmar. From these ports, after it is refined into morphine or heroin, couriers smuggle the drugs into other countries.

After being joined by the Nam Tha, one of its major tributaries, the Mekong widens and becomes navigable by larger sampans and junks. It makes a wide loop and heads east, away from the Thailand border and toward the town of Luang Prabang, where another tributary, the Nam Khan, joins the Mekong. Luang Prabang, once the royal capital (1353–1975), sits on the hilly peninsula between the two rivers.

Luang Prabang was named after the golden statue of Buddha, called the Pra Bang, that was the symbol of Laos and of its king. Before the Communists assumed power in 1975, the Pra Bang was displayed in the royal palace. The features of this solid gold figure, which is about three feet (one meter) tall, are blurred by layers of gold leaf pressed on it by devout pilgrims. Near the center of town a hill called the Phousi is topped by a beautiful *sim*, or Buddhist temple. The curving ridgepoles (the uppermost roof beams) of its shingled roofs are carved in the form of serpents, or *nagas*. The nagas of Laos sometimes look like fearsome dragons, but they are really sacred, benevolent beasts that represent the mythical cobra who once spread his hood over the meditating Buddha to protect him from the rain.

From Luang Prabang the Mekong flows south. The hilly, forested land on the right bank of this 200-mile (333-kilometer) stretch is Sayaboury, the only province of Laos located west of the Mekong. Sayaboury, whose principal town is Pak Lay, is the center of Laos's elephant-training industry. Asian elephants were once plentiful in the upland monsoon forests of Sayaboury, and young animals were trapped and trained to work in logging and construction throughout the Indochina peninsula.

A trained elephant can pick its way through tangled brush to drag giant teak and rosewood logs to a river so that they can be floated to sawmills. An adult female can lift logs weighing a ton (900 kilograms) and can drag as much as 2 tons (1,800 kilograms). Elephant trainers prefer females because they are easier to teach and less unpredictable than males. Elephants are good swimmers, and their drivers can guide them into the swollen rivers to steer rafts of felled trees downstream. Rare white elephants were trained for careers in court as prized symbols of royalty. Asian armies of old used the enormous animals to strike terror into the ranks of opposing infantry.

Even today, a case can be made for the utilization of elephants: A well-cared-for elephant has a longer life expectancy than a truck or bulldozer, and its upkeep is less. Elephants can travel and work in hilly, overgrown terrain, pulling valuable logs out of places that only helicopters could otherwise reach. Elephants are still used in the forests of Thailand, Myanmar, and Laos, but the practice may not endure because the spread of slash-and-burn agriculture throughout the region has reduced the habitat of the Asian elephant. There are still wild elephants in the forests of Laos, but they are too

By giving commands with his voice and bare feet, a handler directs an elephant along a road in the city of Luang Prabang. Although the number of elephants in Laos has dwindled to fewer than 900, some are still used for logging and construction work.

rare to maintain a dependable supply of young animals to be trained.

A few miles south of Pak Lay, the Mekong turns sharply once more and flows northeast, again forming the border between Laos and Thailand. The mountains have subsided into rolling hills along this stretch, and the floodplains are broad and fertile on both sides of the river. As the river passes Vientiane, the capital city, it is divided by Chan Island and fringed on both sides by swamps.

Vientiane is Laos's largest city, with a population of about 442,000. The center of town consists of three parallel streets that run for about a mile behind the waterfront. Several two-story brick and stucco buildings with cast-iron railings—relics of the French colonial

The Nam Ngum dam produces hydroelectric power, most of which is exported to Thailand. The dam, which opened in 1971, controls flooding along the river, and the electricity produced by its power plant provides more than half of Laos's export earnings.

period—remain, but most of the houses stand on stilts and are built of wood and bamboo with plaited thatch roofs.

Buddhist temple compounds, called wats, are located throughout the city. The largest, Wat Pra Keo, still stands on the waterfront next to the former royal residence. Nearby is the 16th-century Buddhist shrine, That Luang. *That* is the Lao word for a stupa, a stone tower or mound, usually hemispherical in shape, built to honor Buddha. That Luang consists of two rows of pointed stupas that form a long avenue leading to a large memorial building, 100 feet (30 meters) tall. Almost every surface of That Luang is covered with intricate carvings. Rigid, stylized figures of gods and humans are surrounded by plants and flowers so intricately intertwined that they almost make an abstract pattern.

East of Vientiane another major tributary, the Nam Ngum, joins the Mekong. In the early 1970s, the United Nations and the United States contributed money and expertise to help Laos build a dam, a power plant, and an irrigation and flood control project on the Nam Ngum. Laos sells most of the electricity produced by the power plant to Thailand, which is just across the river. This is the source of more than half of the country's income from exports.

After meeting the Nam Ngum, the Mekong then curves to the southeast, serving for about 400 miles (645 kilometers) as the western edge of Laos's southern panhandle. To the west is Thailand's vast Khorat Plateau. Between the market towns and fishing villages of Pak Sane and Thakhek, the Annam Cordillera shoulders close to the river valley, so that the tillable stretch of level land on Laos's side of the bank is only a few kilometers wide. Below Thakhek, however, several rivers, including the Bang Fai and the Bang Hieng, flow down from the mountains and join the Mekong, creating broad floodplains. Rice cultivation and human habitation flourish on these deltas.

The largest town in this region is Savannakhet, the principal city of the province with the same name. Savannakhet is Laos's second

Near the village of Khong, waterfalls and huge rocks make the Mekong unnavigable as it flows south toward the Laos-Cambodia border.

largest city, with a population of approximately 53,000. In addition to being a fishing village and market town, Savannakhet is a transportation hub. A major road, heading directly east over a pass in the Annam Cordillera, connects Laos with the sea at Da Nang, Vietnam. Another road leads south to Ubon Ratchathani, Thailand, the terminus of the closest railway to Laos. Savannakhet is also the last Laotian port on the Mekong for the larger sampans and junks. Except during high water, only pirogues can travel the 80-mile (133-kilometer) stretch south of the town. The river changes from a slow waterway that is nearly 5,000 feet (1,500 meters) wide into several swift channels separated by rocky islands.

Near the bottom of the panhandle, the Thai border once more draws away from the Mekong, leaving a small triangular patch of fertile lowlands on the west side of the river within Laos. The town of Pakse sits on the east bank, and the village of Champasak lies among the paddies on the west. Farther south, at the village of Khong, huge rocks interrupt the river's flow again. The Mekong cascades over the rocks in several waterfalls. Each of the two main falls is over 50 feet (15 meters) high. Below the falls the river once again divides into several branches, rushing past small, lushly forested islands before it enters Cambodia.

The Mountain Plateaus

The only level areas in Laos besides the floodplains are its mountain plateaus. A plateau is a flat expanse of land that is higher than adjacent terrain. The largest is the Tran Ninh Plateau, located in the northern province of Xiangkhoang. Tran Ninh is a broad stretch of plains and rolling hills with an average altitude of 3,900 feet (1,190 meters). Phou Bia, Laos's highest mountain (9,250 feet, or 2,820 meters) rises along its southern edge. The soil of Tran Ninh is poor, and most of the land is treeless, covered with scrub or tall grasses.

Near the center of the Tran Ninh Plateau is a plain covered with grass and scattered trees. This is the Plain of Jars, which is named for the giant stone vessels shaped like pitchers (in French, *jarres*) found buried there. Each jar, weighing 4,000 to 6,000 pounds (1,800 to 2,700 kilograms), was carved from a single piece of stone of a kind

A Laotian youth examines one of the many large stone vessels scattered across the Plain of Jars. This area, located in the center of the Tran Ninh Plateau, is named after the pitcher-shaped stones found there. Archaeologists can only speculate about the origin and function of the vessels.

not indigenous to the area. Archaeologists do not know who carved the jars and put them in place or what purpose, if any, they served. Were they burial urns? Or did their makers store rice in them? Some believe that the Plain of Jars was the wine cellar of a vanished civilization.

In the neck of the panhandle, the Cammon Plateau runs between the Mekong River and the Annam Cordillera. Limestone hills, eroded into fantastic shapes and smothered in lush greenery, loom out of the mist. Rivers have cut steep-sided gorges through the porous limestone; in places, they disappear underground, where they flow through cavernous grottoes. Geologists call this kind of terrain karst.

Farther south is the Bolovens Plateau, which has an average elevation of 3,500 feet (1,070 meters). It is a vast bowl of approximately 26,000 square miles (10,000 square kilometers), almost completely ringed by sheer mountains. Fertile soil, abundant rain, and the cooler upland air make the Bolovens Plateau one of the most productive agricultural regions in Laos. Besides rice, the plateau supports commercial crops such as peaches, pears, pineapples, and tobacco.

Rubber and coffee plantations flourished here during the French colonial period. Before the invention of synthetic rubber and plastic substitutes, rubber was vital to the industrialized nations and their mechanized armed forces. It was partly to secure rubber from the Bolovens Plateau and other regions that Japan invaded the Indochina peninsula at the outbreak of World War II. That invasion initiated 35 years of almost continuous conflict for Laos. By 1975, the coffee and rubber plantations of the Bolovens Plateau had succumbed to the effects of bombing and neglect. Since then, Laos has revived its coffee production to a point at which the export of coffee is a significant source of income for its struggling economy, but its rubber plantations have not been restored.

Plant and Animal Life

Even though 80 percent of all Laotians are farmers, only about 4 percent of all the land in Laos is cultivated. Roughly 60 percent of the country is still covered with forest. Tropical rain forests flourish in the areas with high rainfall and year-round humidity, mostly in the north and the mountains of the panhandle. Monsoon forest covers most of the rest of the mountains and hills of Laos. Stands of pines and birch flourish in Sayaboury and the northern provinces of Phong Saly and Sam Neua.

Tropical rain forests are the earth's richest and most varied ecosystems. They contain thousands of species of broad-leaved evergreen trees, vines, and shrubs. Their broad canopies and shadowed understories are home to hundreds of varieties of reptiles, amphibians, and birds, untold numbers of insect species, and a wide variety of mammals, including primates, humankind's nearest relatives. Most rain forest trees are 85 to 110 feet (26 to 34 meters) tall. They have straight trunks, and their branches grow only at the top. Their spreading crowns crowd against each other in a layer of green called the canopy. The tops of smaller, shade-tolerant trees create a second tier of foliage about 45 to 60 feet (14 to 18 meters) high, which is called the understory.

Not much sunlight passes through the canopy and understory, so the shadowy floor of the forest is relatively free of undergrowth. When a tree dies and falls, smaller vegetation springs up where the sunlight breaks through the leafy roof. Where the forest grows on slopes, as in the mountains of Laos, more sunlight reaches the lower levels, producing luxuriant carpets of ferns.

Seen from above, the rain forest presents an unbroken green surface, punctuated by occasional taller trees called emergents. One emergent, the tapang, can reach the height of 250 feet (75 meters). From within, the rain forest resembles a steamy, dim cathedral. No breezes move through the understory. Stray beams of sunlight stream across the open spaces between the ground cover and the foliage layers. The trunks of trees are like columns holding up a green vaulted ceiling. The trunk of the tapang is especially impressive; it is supported by large ribs, or buttresses, for the first 30 feet (9 meters) or so; these taper off to a trunk about 10 feet (3 meters) in diameter that leaps straight up for 80 to 100 feet (24 to 30 meters) before branching.

Staghorn ferns flourish on tree trunks, and the brilliant purple and red flowers of the bougainvillea vine glow in the branches. Giant lianas and other vines hang from the understory in shaggy green loops. Orchids grow on branches high in the canopy, where their extravagant blossoms attract the insects that carry pollen from flower to flower.

Besides hardwood trees, such as oaks, pines, and hornbeams, many kinds of palm trees grow in the rain forest. Some trees, such as the coconut palm, the betel palm, and the banana (which is actually not a tree at all but a giant herb with palmlike fronds), are also under cultivation in villages and on plantations. The coconut palm is one of the most useful plants in Laos. Its seed, the coconut, is a source of rich white meat and the nutritious liquid called coconut milk. Copra, dried coconut meat, is an important export product for other Southeast Asian countries and could be important for Laos's future. Processing copra yields coconut oil, which is used in cooking and food processing in developed countries. The husks of the nut provide fiber for ropes and mats, and its leaves are used for thatching roofs and weaving baskets.

The seed of the betel palm, the betel nut, contains a mild narcotic. For centuries the people of Southeast Asia have chewed thin slices of betel nut for the mild "high" it produces. Betel chewers are easy to spot because their lips, gums, and teeth are stained dark.

Pitcher plants abound on the jungle floor. The pitcher is a funnel-shaped vessel formed by the plant's leaf. Some pitchers mimic the shape and color of flowers attractive to insects. The leaf secretes an enzyme that collects at the bottom of the pitcher. Insects attracted

by the flowerlike shape or odor slip on the waxy rim of the pitcher, fall in, and drown. They dissolve in the enzyme as the plant slowly digests them.

Each layer of the rain forest is a distinct microclimate. The wind blows through the treetops but does not reach the lower levels, so the canopy layer is less humid than the ground level or understory. The temperature varies more in the canopy too, in response to the rhythm of sunlight and dark. Each microclimate supports its own

A concave-casqued hornbill perches majestically on a tree branch. Several species of hornbills are among the many exotic birds that live in the jungles of Laos.

fauna. For instance, some species of tree shrews live exclusively on the ground, while others remain in the canopy. Some tree frogs live their whole life in the canopy. They have evolved so that, unlike most frogs, they do not even need to lay their eggs in water.

Butterflies of the rain forest grow much larger wings than species in other parts of the world because there is little wind to hinder their flight. The variety of butterflies and other insects is staggering. Among the more remarkable are the long-horned beetles (more than 1,000 species), some with 6-inch (15-centimeter) bodies. Their horns are actually antennae that are up to three times longer than their bodies.

The sexton beetles, named after the official who often digs graves in a churchyard, bury the bodies of small animals, such as mice, by carrying away the soil beneath them. Before covering a corpse, they lay their eggs in its flesh, ensuring a source of food for the larvae.

Birds abound in both the canopy and the understory. Many different species sweep through the jungle in feeding flocks. These noisy processions are usually started by the raucous cries of drongos, robin-sized birds with shiny blue-black plumage and long tails. Warblers, babblers, hornbills, and bulbuls join the flock, each species adding its own distinctive calls.

The hornbill is one of the most striking birds in the Laotian rain forest. Its plumage is black or brown, with large patches of white or yellow. Some hornbills have bright red patches of bare skin, like the turkey's wattles, above the eye and throat. Hornbills have a large, colorful beak. In the male (and, in some species, the female), the horny material of the beak extends back and over the head like a helmet, or casque, which acts as an echo chamber for the bird's loud, hoarse call.

Many snakes also live in the rain forest, some on the ground, some in the trees. The python haunts the banks of streams, waiting to dart at its prey, seize it with its teeth, and crush it in the coils of its body. The reticulated python, the world's largest snake, can reach a length of 30 feet (9 meters) and is capable of devouring a small deer. The flying snake, which does not really fly but is said by some to be able to glide, coils itself on top of a branch before throwing itself off. Once aloft, the snake straightens out and draws in its stomach, giving it a slightly concave undersurface that may act to trap a cushion of air and provide some lift. However, the effect is small, and the snake's flight is more of a controlled fall than a glide. Gliding is an accomplishment shared by several rain forest animals, including several species of lizards and squirrels.

The most impressive glider of all is the colugo, a gray-green lemur about the size of a house cat. Lemurs are primates, part of the order of mammals that includes monkeys, apes, and humans. The colugo has webs between its neck and forelegs, between its legs, and even between its rear legs and tail. The folds of fur-covered membrane that hang from the colugo give it a grotesque look as it climbs awkwardly through the branches of the canopy. When it leaps into the air and spreads its limbs, however, the colugo can glide more than 200 feet (61 meters).

Several kinds of monkeys live in the canopy and understory. They rove in noisy troops, swinging and jumping from branch to branch. Gibbons roam the treetops in search of food. These small apes are well adapted to life in the canopy. Their arms are very long and very strong, and they are capable of prodigious leaps as they swing along high above the jungle floor. Unlike monkeys, who live and travel in packs, gibbons are fiercely territorial animals who live in permanent families of one male, one female, and their offspring.

Another tree-dwelling primate is the slow loris. This tiny (about 12 inches, or 30 centimeters, long), long-limbed climber has plush fur, a short tail, and rounded ears. The loris, like other primates, has well-developed paws with grasping digits that resemble human hands. Like other nocturnal animals, it has large oval eyes, giving it the endearing look of a child's stuffed animal.

Wild pigs and several kinds of deer are among the larger mammals of the Laotian rain forest. They provide sustenance for the most magnificent inhabitant of the jungle, the tiger. Tigers are the largest of the great cats and once roamed throughout India and Southeast Asia. Because of pressure from humans, there are very

A Laotian farmer extinguishes smoldering embers in a small plot that he has cleared in a forest. By cutting down trees and burning them—a method known as slash-and-burn agriculture—the farmer will be able to plant rice, corn, and other crops. Slash-and-burn agriculture is common in Laos.

few of these nocturnal, solitary creatures left. In Laos, they have retreated to the wildest and most remote parts of the rain forest. There, they feed on wild pigs and several kinds of deer.

Leopards live in both rain forest and monsoon forest. Smaller than the tiger, the leopard lies in wait in the lower branches of the trees and leaps on its prey from above. Most leopards have yellow fur patterned with black spots and rings. The panther, which lives in the mountains of the Annam Cordillera, is a leopard with an almost completely black coat.

Monsoon forests thrive in regions that are not wet enough year-round to support rain forests. Many of the same trees, such as oak, maple, and hornbeam, grow in both environments. In monsoon forests, however, these hardwoods are deciduous; that is, they drop all their leaves at one time. In temperate climates, deciduous trees shed their foliage in the fall and grow new leaves in spring. In the tropics, the trees of the monsoon forest shed in January, the beginning of the dry season, and are bare until the rains come again in May. The trees in the rain forests are evergreens; their dying leaves drop one at a time, and new ones replace them immediately, throughout the year.

Monsoon forest is much more open than rain forest. The trees are smaller, about 45 to 65 feet (14 to 20 meters) tall. Their crowns are separate, or barely touching, and there are open spaces in the foliage layer. Imperata grass grows as high as six feet (two meters) on the forest floor in places. Other parts of the forest floor are covered with thick, thorny underbrush. Because dry conditions produce denser, harder wood, the teak, sandalwood, and rosewood trees of the monsoon forest are more valuable commercially than those of the rain forest. Commercial logging is not yet as important an industry in Laos as in neighboring Myanmar and Thailand.

Hill farmers find monsoon forest easier than rain forest to clear by the slash-and-burn method, which destroys valuable timber and sometimes irreplaceable natural habitats. When the soil is exhausted and the farmers move on, the barren fields are taken over by dense groves of bamboo or become choked with bushy scrub.

Many of the same animals live in both rain forest and monsoon forest. Life is not so wildly abundant and varied, however, in the monsoon forest ecosystem. Fewer vines drape the trees, and there are no orchids in the upper foliage. There are fewer insects and,

A gaur grazes in a Laotian forest. The gaur, a species of wild ox, can weigh more than 2,200 pounds (1,000 kilograms).

therefore, fewer birds and other insect predators, such as lizards and frogs.

The hoopoe is one of the more plentiful birds in Laos's monsoon forests. About the size of a jay, the hoopoe has a reddish brown body and bold black and white stripes on its wings and tail. Long, pinkish brown feathers tipped with black lie back along the top of the male's head. When he is excited, or courting, he raises these into a very handsome crest. The hoopoe's bill is long, slender, and downcurved, adapted to probing the ground for insects and spiders. The bill is so long and narrow that there is no room for a tongue. The hoopoe tosses its head back and throws its captured grub or beetle into the air, catching dinner in its widely opened mouth.

Huge wild oxen, called gaurs, are, next to the elephant, the largest animals in the monsoon forest. An adult gaur may stand over 6 feet (2 meters) high at the shoulder and weigh over 2,200 pounds (1,000 kilograms). Gaurs have long horns that sweep back and down from their brow. When they want to frighten an opponent, such as a tiger, they approach it sideways, perhaps to impress it with their bulk. Gaurs travel in herds of up to 20. They feed in meadows and open glades but never stray far from the refuge of the forest.

Many other different plants and animals thrive in Laos. Bears live in the northern forest, and wild buffalo appear on some of the upland plains. The rivers teem with carp, catfish, perch, and many other fish. Herons and egrets stalk the fish in shallows and marshes. Cranes, ducks, and partridges fill the air. Rare Siamese crocodiles once lurked in the upper reaches of the Mekong, and the even rarer Sumatran rhinoceros could once be found in the mountain jungles along the Vietnam border. Both crocodiles and rhinoceroses are thought to be extinct in Laos, casualties of prolonged warfare and the intense bombing in their home ranges.

*That Luang, a Buddhist shrine, was erected by Sethathirath, king (1547–71) of the an-
cient empire of Lan Xang. Lan Xang, which in Lao means "the land of the million
elephants," covered much of the Indochina peninsula, including present-day Laos.*

3

The Land of the Million Elephants

The history of Laos begins with Fa Ngum. In 1353 he became king of a Tai-Lao principality on the Mekong that he transformed into Lan Xang, literally "the land of the million elephants." The son of a Tai-Lao prince who sent him to live at the court of the Khmer emperor in Angkor (in the northwest of present-day Cambodia), Fa Ngum married one of the emperor's daughters and converted to Buddhism, a major religion of eastern and central Asia. When his father died, Fa Ngum became ruler of the small Lao kingdom. In spite of the pacifist nature of his new religion, Fa Ngum was a mighty warrior. With the help of his father-in-law, he extended his rule until Lan Xang included all of present-day Laos, much of what is now northeast Thailand, and parts of Vietnam and China.

Fa Ngum made Buddhism the official religion, although it never fully replaced the spirit worship of the area's earliest inhabitants. Influenced by and dependent upon the Khmer Empire, Fa Ngum helped spread the Indian-Khmer culture through the northcentral part of the Indochina peninsula. One of the many gifts of the Khmer to Fa Ngum was the Pra Bang, the golden statue of Buddha that became a symbol of Lan Xang and the monarchy. The king built a large wat to house the statue at his capital, Muong Swa. The statue is so important to the Lao sense of identity that a hundred years later one of Fa Ngum's successors changed the name of the capital to Luang Prabang, "Royal Home of the Pra Bang."

For all of his success, Fa Ngum's militarism angered his subjects. In 1373 he was deposed and was succeeded by his son, Sam Sene Thai. The new king consolidated his father's conquests into a stable kingdom. He encouraged the spread of Buddhism and constructed many wats throughout the new lands. The government that Sam Sene Thai built was based on the principle of absolute monarchy. All officials, tax collectors, and judges held their jobs entirely at the king's pleasure. All the positions of power were held by members of the royal family. One innovation unique to Laos was the *maha oupahat*, or second king, who was the king's closest adviser and usually his son or heir. The maha oupahat took over many of the king's ceremonial duties and at times ruled in the king's absence.

Sam Sene Thai's name meant "Lord of 300,000 Tai," which was the number of Tai-Lao in his kingdom, according to a census the

Three worshipers pray before the Pra Bang, a solid gold statue of Buddha. The Pra Bang— which was given to Fa Ngum, the first ruler of Lan Xang, by the Khmers —was the symbol of the kingdom. The royal capital, Luang Prabang, was named after the statue.

king ordered in 1376. He had a standing army of 150,000 men, including infantry and a cavalry with war elephants. As Lan Xang rose, the Khmer Empire declined, until by the end of Sam Sene Thai's reign in 1416 Lan Xang dominated the region. It controlled a vast territory, but the Lao population was fairly small. Lan Xang benefited from the involvement of its neighbors in conflicts among themselves or with outsiders. The neighboring state of Annam (now Vietnam), for instance, was involved in a war with China. For a hundred years, except for an Annamese invasion in 1478, the Lao kings of Lan Xang ruled in comparative peace and prosperity.

This happy state of affairs was upset when King Photisarath (1520–47) tried to extend Lan Xang's power by placing his son Sethathirath on the throne of nearby Chiengmai (in present-day Thailand). This offended the neighboring kingdom of Siam and prompted the king of Burma to become involved in the dispute. Forty years of three-way conflict followed.

Sethathirath succeeded his father and ruled Lan Xang from 1547 to 1571. Although he lost Chiengmai to Burma, he repelled two Burmese invasions of Lan Xang and for a time improved relations with Siam. To be closer to the center of trade and foreign relations, Sethathirath moved the capital to Vientiane. He brought the fabulous Emerald Buddha (Pra Keo) from Chiengmai and installed it in a newly constructed temple, Wat Pra Keo. Nearby he built an even larger shrine, That Luang, to hold sacred relics of Buddha.

Sethathirath disappeared during an expedition against rebellious hill tribes in 1571. Three years later, the Burmese finally defeated Lan Xang's armies and ravaged the country. In 1591, Siam attacked Burma, enabling Lan Xang to declare independence. The country was still weak, however, and lacked a strong ruler. Sethathirath's son died without an heir, and for many years various factions of the royal family fought for control of the monarchy. It took Lan Xang almost 100 years to reestablish itself.

In 1637, Souligna Vongsa won a power struggle and seized the crown. During his long reign (1637–94), Souligna Vongsa restored Lan Xang's power and secured its borders by treaties with Annam and Siam. Under Souligna Vongsa, Lan Xang reached its peak in terms of land area and prosperity. Crops were bountiful, and the king established many temples. Laotians still look back on his reign as the Golden Age.

The first Europeans arrived during this period. In 1641 a Dutch merchant named Gerrit van Wuysthoff led a delegation from the governor of the Dutch West Indies in search of trade in forest products and spices. Van Wuysthoff was impressed by the king, who, carried on a throne of gold, led a procession of cavalry, war elephants, and musketeers through the capital. The Dutchman also noted that bonzes, or Buddhist monks, were "more numerous than the soldiers of the Emperor of Germany." Later, a French Jesuit came to Lan Xang to start a mission. The bonzes were hospitable, and the people were friendly, but nobody was very interested in the Christian god. After about five years the Jesuit grew discouraged and left.

Things fell apart quickly after Souligna Vongsa's death. The king had made two serious mistakes. He had alienated the rulers of Xieng Khouang, a small, dependent kingdom on the border with Annam, when he fell in love with a Xieng Khouang princess and carried her off by force. Second, he executed his only son for adultery, leaving no adult heir to his throne.

The old king's death began a fight over who was to succeed him. Xieng Khouang took advantage of the confusion to declare independence. Meanwhile, one of Souligna Vongsa's nephews, who had been exiled in Annam, seized the throne of Lan Xang with the help of an Annamese army. In return, he agreed to accept orders from the Annamese king and to pay an enormous yearly tribute. Other members of the royal family rebelled, and Lan Xang split into three smaller, weaker states.

In 1707, Souligna Vongsa's grandson Kisarath was established as ruler of Luang Prabang, in the north. Six years later, another member of the royalty carved the kingdom of Champasak out of southern Lan Xang, which included the rich land on both sides of the lower Mekong. What was left of Lan Xang—territory on both sides of the middle Mekong—became the kingdom of Vientiane under the control of Souligna Vongsa's nephew.

For the next 150 years, these fragments of the great Lao kingdom of Lan Xang were caught between the ambitions of Siam, Burma, and Annam. From its beginnings, Champasak was more or less a Siamese dependency. Luang Prabang was invaded in 1752 by the Burmese, who ruled until the Siamese drove them out in 1778. In the same year Siam invaded and occupied Vientiane. Vientiane expelled Siam with help from the Annamese emperor in 1802 but soon found itself paying tribute to both countries. Xieng Khouang, too, maintained a precarious independence by paying tribute to Annam.

In the 1820s the throne of Vientiane was held by Prince Anou, who tried to escape Siamese domination by signing a treaty with Annam. In 1826, after the British conquered Burma, Anou was convinced that they would invade Siam. He led his army on a march against Bangkok, Siam's capital, but was beaten back. Siamese troops then swept over Vientiane in 1829. They destroyed the capital and carried the Pra Keo (Emerald Buddha) to Bangkok. The victors drove the surviving Lao across the river into Siam. For many years the middle Mekong region was almost deserted as Siamese and Annamese armies swept across the land in periodic invasions and counterinvasions.

By the 1880s, Vientiane and Xieng Khouang were again ruled by Siam. Luang Prabang had lost much of its territory to Siam and Annam and was reduced to a powerless buffer between the two stronger kingdoms. The Lao principalities, heirs to the glory of Lan Xang, had almost been squeezed out of existence.

Three soldiers who represent different factions trying to establish a firm government in Laos—(left to right) the royal government, the neutralist party, and the Communist-backed Pathet Lao—stand guard during a peace conference held in Vientiane in 1961.

4

The Protectorate and Independence

The French intrusion into the Indochina peninsula changed the balance of power. They annexed Cochin China (what is now northern Vietnam) in 1864 and established protectorates in Annam and Tonkin (central and southern Vietnam, respectively) as well as Cambodia. "Protectorate" is a polite term for colony. Each protectorate had native rulers, but the French, who organized the land and the labor force to benefit themselves, held the real power.

Siam suddenly changed from an expanding empire to a state threatened by French invasion from the east and British pressure from the west. Now the lone kingdom in the region, Siam remained independent but was forced to relinquish its control of the Lao principalities to France. In 1886, France sent a representative, Auguste Pavie, to Luang Prabang. The escalating French presence on the Mekong led to clashes between French and Siamese troops. In 1893 the French navy blockaded Bangkok, and in the face of superior military strength, Siam ceded Luang Prabang to the French.

In 1904 and 1907 the French forced Siam to forfeit all of its remaining claims to the east bank of the Mekong. In return, Siam gained undisputed title to the more fertile west bank, which was once held by the Lao kings of Lan Xang. In effect, the borders of Siam, Laos, Vietnam, and Cambodia were determined by the French, who made their decisions according to what they could squeeze out of the Siamese and how they were going to administer the new territory. The history of the land and the ethnic composition of the population was ignored. This shortsighted division of ancient lands would lead to much bloodshed when the colonies later won their independence.

The French occupation of Laos proved peaceful for both Laotians and the French. The French recognized the royal title and prerogatives of the king of Luang Prabang, Sisavang Vong, and ruled through him. The rest of the new territory that would eventually become Laos was ruled directly by the French resident (representative) in Vientiane, with the assistance of Vietnamese administrators. The French left the local power structure in place and confined their direct control to fiscal matters, especially tax collecting. They respected native social institutions, with the exception of slavery, which they banned.

The protectorate of Laos was not, however, very profitable for the French. The Mekong, because of its unnavigable rapids, was not an international trade route. Monsoon rains washed out the roads every year, making it difficult to organize plantations and to get agricultural products to market. Only a very portable, high-value crop, such as opium, was profitable. Some historians maintain that the French managed to pay most of the costs of running the protectorate out of their proceeds from the opium trade.

French administrators worked to improve sanitation and public health throughout Laos. They had only partial success in the cities and towns and almost none at all in the rural villages. Attempts to establish a countrywide educational system followed the same pattern. The French colonial efforts were interrupted by World War I and then were slowed down considerably by the worldwide depression of the 1930s.

In 1940, at the outset of World War II, the Japanese occupied the Indochina peninsula. Because Germany, an ally of Japan, controlled the French government during its occupation of France (1940–44), the Japanese left the French administration in place. Officially, the German-backed Vichy government of France controlled the French colonies. Nevertheless, it was apparent to everyone in Asia that the Japanese were really running things. The myth of European invincibility crumbled, and the end of French rule became inevitable.

In 1941, Japan returned to Thailand some of the land that the French had forced the Thais to cede to Laos in 1904. Japan then consolidated the various remaining provinces under the rule of King Sisavang Vong, in effect unifying Laos. The king's eldest son and maha oupahat, Prince Phetsereth, became prime minister.

But four years later, facing defeat in the Pacific, Japan ousted the French and declared Laos an independent country. At first the king tried to remain loyal to France, but the Japanese forced him to declare complete independence. Even so, many in the ruling class, which was made up predominantly of members of the royal family, still favored resumption of French rule. Prince Phetsereth did not. He helped to form a group called Lao Issara (Free Lao) to resist the return of the French. The revolutionary Vietminh (Free Vietnam) under Ho Chi Minh offered support. French paratroopers, however, seized control of Laos in the summer of 1945. In October the king, pressured by the French, stripped Prince Phetsereth of his position as prime minister. The prince and other members of the Lao Issara fled to Thailand, where they declared themselves the government-in-exile.

After a year of political and military maneuvering, Sisavang Vong was crowned king of a unified Laos in 1946, and the French agreed to negotiate with Laotian representatives concerning indepen-

In October 1953, King Sisavang Vong of Laos (left) joins French officials in signing a Laotian-French treaty of friendship in Paris. The agreement was the first step toward Laos's independence, which was achieved the following year.

dence. Later that year, elected delegates to a national assembly produced a constitution, which the king declared the law of the land in May 1947. The constitution provided for national elections but left many powers to the monarchy. The king commanded the armed forces and appointed the prime minister, who was the head of the government.

In 1949, France declared Laos an independent kingdom within the French Union. The French Union was a last-ditch effort to hold on to the colonies of Laos, Vietnam, and Cambodia by allowing them limited self-rule. It was too late for that, however. The idea of national independence had swept over Southeast Asia. The Vietminh controlled the northern half of Vietnam, and revolutionary guerilla forces operated throughout southern Vietnam, Laos, and Cambodia. The Lao Issara had accepted the new government, but some Laotians demanded complete independence. They formed the Pathet Lao (Lao Country), which with Vietminh assistance fought royal government troops and French forces in the northeastern mountains.

The French found themselves challenged on all fronts. From 1945 to 1954, they fought a losing battle, known as the First Indochina War, against the forces of independence. French resolve finally broke after the siege of Dien Bien Phu. In a valley in the mountains of northern Vietnam, the Vietminh surrounded the last effective French army in the region and starved it into surrender. After Dien Bien Phu, the French agreed to participate in an international peace conference in Geneva, Switzerland.

Independence

The 1954 Geneva Peace Agreement gave Laos and Cambodia full independence. As constitutional monarchies, they were to remain neutral, with no allegiance to either West or East. The agreement also divided Vietnam in half. North Vietnam was ruled by the Communist Vietminh under Ho Chi Minh, and South Vietnam was established as a pro-Western state. The agreement also called for Vietnamese elections in 1956 that would reunite the country under one form of government.

The peace agreement soon collapsed—another case of the failure of European solutions to Asian problems. A civil war began in South Vietnam that soon developed into another areawide conflict, known as the Second Indochina (or Vietnam) War (1955–75). By 1965, the United States sent troops to South Vietnam and began bombing North Vietnam. American involvement escalated, despite growing opposition to the war in the United States.

Laos became involved in the conflict at an early stage. After the 1954 agreement, Prince Souvanna Phouma formed a coalition government with his half brother, Prince Souphanouvong, leader of the Pathet Lao. But 1958 elections showed gains by the Communist Pathet Lao. This alarmed the pro-Western party, and in 1959 they forced Souvanna Phouma out of office and formed a new government, which may have been aided by agents of the U.S. Central Intelligence Agency (CIA). The new leaders arrested Prince Souphanouvong in May 1959 and accepted U.S. military aid. This violation of neutrality prompted the Pathet Lao to resort once more to armed conflict. With North Vietnamese help, they seized control of the northeastern provinces and expelled the officials of the U.S.-backed government.

The United States intervened in Laos because it wanted military access to Laos on account of the Ho Chi Minh trail, the American name for a network of trails and roads that North Vietnam used to transport troops and supplies from Hanoi through the eastern mountains of Laos to South Vietnam. The United States wanted to stop North Vietnam's aid to the Vietcong (the guerilla group that opposed South Vietnam's government) by destroying the trail in Laos. Although American planes rained tons of bombs into the jungles of Laos, they were never able to close the trail.

Meanwhile, Laos plunged into civil war. The government became paralyzed by the struggle between the Left and the Right. There were fraudulent elections, coups, and countercoups. Pathet Lao and neutralist forces, supported by the Soviet Union, fought with royal government forces supported by the United States. Ultimately, the threat of world war compelled the superpowers to seek peace.

In 1961, the Geneva Peace Conference reconvened, and all parties once again pledged to respect Laotian neutrality. But neither the United States nor North Vietnam intended to give up its interests in the war-torn nation. Until 1973, the United States pursued a "secret war" in Laos. During each dry season, Pathet Lao and North Vietnamese forces stormed out of the Communist-controlled areas in the north and east in attempts to gain control of the cities. In the rainy season, when U.S. airpower gave them the advantage, royal

North Vietnamese soldiers carry supplies along the Ho Chi Minh trail in Laos. The Ho Chi Minh trail was a network of trails and roads used by North Vietnam to transport military supplies to forces in South Vietnam during the Vietnam War (1955–75).

government forces pushed the Communists back. American jets continued to bombard the jungles that concealed the Ho Chi Minh trail.

The main theater of the war was in South Vietnam. United States and South Vietnamese forces failed to defeat the Vietcong and North Vietnamese armies in South Vietnam. The United States began recalling American troops in 1970, although they stepped up the bombing of North Vietnam and invaded both Laos and Cambodia to destroy Communist strongholds in those countries. North Vietnam and the United States reached a cease-fire agreement in 1973, and the United States began a complete withdrawal from Southeast Asia. South Vietnam fell to North Vietnamese armies in April 1975, and the U.S.-supported government of Cambodia fell to the Communist Khmer Rouge, which renamed the country Kampuchea. In June 1975, the Pathet Lao seized Vientiane.

The Lao People's Democratic Republic

In December 1975, King Savang Vatthana abdicated, and the Pathet Lao seized power and proclaimed Laos a socialist republic, renaming it the Lao People's Democratic Republic. Prince Souphanouvong became chairman of the People's Assembly, but the real head of the government was Prime Minister Kaysone Phomvihane, a longtime leader of the Communist rebels and a protégé of Ho Chi Minh's.

The king and about 30,000 former government officials were sent to "political reeducation" camps, where they were forced to work in the fields and taught to honor, at least publicly, the ideals and principles of the new regime. Instead of submitting to the new order, many Laotians fled to Thailand.

At first, the Pathet Lao regime depended heavily on economic and military aid from Vietnam. Until 1988, about 40,000 Vietnamese troops remained stationed in Laos, and many observers felt that Vietnam was essentially controlling the Laotian state.

During this early period, Laos's ruling party, the Lao People's Revolutionary party (LPRP), encountered difficulty in improving conditions in the desperately poor country. Throughout the late 1970s, for instance, severe flooding along the Mekong and its tributaries created economic hardship and dislocation.

By the late 1980s, however, Laos had made significant strides. Programs to develop education and public health systems achieved moderate success. Relations with Thailand improved despite several border clashes over disputed territory. The ties binding Laos to Vietnam gradually loosened, and in 1988 Vietnam withdrew its troops. By the late 1980s, the Laotian government's commitment to socialism was also being modified. Laws restricting private trade and foreign investment were relaxed, and nearly half of the 300 state-owned and -operated manufacturing plants were converted into independently operated en-

On March 26, 1989, Laotian women mark their ballot during the first national election in Laos since 1975. The candidates are pictured on the placards above the voters.

terprises. A new constitution adopted in 1991 deleted all references to socialism. In 1995 Laos announced that it wanted to join the Association of Southeast Asian Nations (ASEAN), an organization dedicated to economic and social development, and the United States decided to lift its ban on aid to Laos.

Despite these moves toward economic liberalization, the Pathet Lao regime stayed firmly in power. Officially Laos remained a one-party state. A national assembly was elected, but the LPRP held 100 percent of the seats.

A Lao Soung woman and child wear traditional clothing. Laos is populated by 68 tribes and ethnic minorities, which are classified into 4 ethnic groups: the Lao Lum, the Lao Tai, the Lao Theung, and the Lao Soung.

5

People and Culture

The original inhabitants of Laos are believed to have come from Indonesia more than 10,000 years ago. Subsequent waves of migration carried several different ethnic groups into Laos, and each was influenced by exposure to other cultures, primarily those of India and China. Ethnic groups are composed of people who share a culture—consisting of language, history, religion, and customs—that is distinct from other cultures. Laos has four main ethnic groups, which are distributed across the country according to altitude. The largest group is the Lao Lum, or valley Lao, who inhabit the Mekong Valley. The Lao Tai, or tribal Tai, live in the upland river valleys. The Lao Theung occupy the mountainsides, and the Lao Soung live at the highest elevations.

The Lao Lum

The Lao Lum, who call themselves simply the Lao, are a subgroup of the Tai people. The Tai once occupied most of what is now southern China, appearing in Chinese records as early as 600 B.C. The Tai kingdom of Nan Chao held sway over what is now the Chinese province of Yunnan from the beginning of the 9th century until the 13th century. Under pressure from the Chinese and later the Mongols, the Tai gradually migrated southward into the Indochina peninsula. Over a period of about 400 years, bands of Tai moved down the valleys of the Irrawaddy, Salween, Chao Phraya, and Mekong rivers. They settled in the fertile lowlands, displacing the earlier inhabitants. Over the centuries, these different migratory groups evolved into the Shan (who now live in Myanmar), the Thai (Thailand), and the Lao (Thailand and Laos). The Lao were among the last to move into the region. They arrived in a surge of migration caused by the fall of Nan Chao in 1253 at the hands of the Mongol warlord Kublai Khan.

Before they came to the Indochina peninsula, the Lao had already learned the techniques of wet-rice agriculture from the Chinese. They knew how to impound the monsoon floodwaters behind dikes and use the water to flood fields (paddies) on the plains and on terraced hillsides. Rice grown in paddies with its roots in water for much of the growing season is called wet rice. It yields much more grain than rice grown in unflooded soil (dry rice). The Lao also learned mastery of the crossbow and other military arts from the Chinese. They gained control of the floodplains of the Mekong, and the former inhabitants, ancestors of today's Lao Theung, retreated into the mountains. During this time, the area was a remote territory of the Khmer Empire, whose capital was Angkor.

The Lao Lum make up nearly half the population of Laos. Before the upheaval of war sent refugees fleeing in many directions, most Laotians living in the towns and cities were Lao Lum, though the urban population included Chinese and Vietnamese minorities. Most Lao Lum, however, continue to live in villages of from 100 to 200 people spread along the edges of their lowland rice paddies.

As the dominant ethnic group in Laos, the Lao Lum have had the most to do with forming the nation's institutions and traditions. The king of Laos, who abdicated in 1975 when the Communist party seized control of the country, was a Lao Lum. The very small ruling class were all members of the royal family, and almost all of the educated elite were also Lao Lum. Lao remains the official lan-

Two Lao Lum women plant rice seedlings in a flooded paddy. Most Lao Lum groups live along the Mekong and its tributaries. They use floodwaters that have overrun the riverbanks to irrigate their fields.

guage, and Buddhism, the religion of the Lao Lum, was the state religion of Laos for more than 700 years, until the country came under Communist rule in 1975.

Buddhism

Buddhism, a religion observed by approximately 250 million people worldwide, provides the foundation of basic beliefs, values, and philosophy for most of the people of Laos. The Lao Lum and some Lao Tai practice Theravada Buddhism, the more conservative branch of one of the world's major religions. Despite the efforts of the ruling Communist party to de-emphasize religion, Buddhism remains one of the most important social forces in Laos.

In the 6th century B.C., Siddhārtha Gautama (ca. 563 – ca. 483 B.C.), an Indian prince, gave up his inherited wealth and status to become a wandering monk. Gautama was a Brahman, a member of the highest caste (class) in India and a priest of the ancient Indian religion, Hinduism. Hindus worship several divine beings that represent various aspects of existence, such as life, growth, and death. They believe that everyone and everything that dies is reincarnated in another form, in an endless cycle of suffering, death, and rebirth.

The goal of Hinduism is to escape the wheel of life, which in Gautama's time meant living correctly in each incarnation by accepting one's lot in life and making the proper prayers and sacrifices. If a person did so, after death he or she would be reborn in a higher caste. Eventually, the person would be incarnated as a Brahman and finally have the chance to escape the wheel of life and achieve unity with the divine.

By fasting, praying, and meditating, Gautama reached a new understanding, called his enlightenment. Gautama became known as Buddha, which means "the Enlightened One" in Sanskrit, an ancient Indian language. He neither claimed divine guidance nor rejected the Hindu principle of reincarnation. Buddha merely expressed a new vision of the nature of life in the Four Noble Truths: existence is suffering; the cause of suffering is desire, or the "thirst" for existence; the end of desire can be the end of suffering; and there is a way to end desire and attain permanent peace, or nirvana. The path to nirvana is not through animal sacrifice or other rituals but through a simple, disciplined way of living called the Eightfold Path, which entails, among other steps, adopting the right views, having the right intentions, and displaying the right conduct.

The appeal of this new vision was that it gave hope of escape to anyone who followed the Eightfold Path. Buddha's followers spread his teachings after his death. In time, the simple, logical prescription for living became a full-fledged religion, and Buddha came to be worshipped as divine. In the 3rd century B.C., the Indian king Aśoka converted to Buddhism. Under his sponsorship, the religion spread over India and to Ceylon (now Sri Lanka), Tibet, and

(continued on page 73)

SCENES OF
LAOS

Overleaf: *A typical Laotian house stands at the edge of adjoining fields. Laos is a land of great natural beauty, with lush jungles, rugged mountains, and rich river valleys.*

The Mekong River flows through Luang Prabang, the former royal capital of Laos. Luang Prabang, an important river port and trading center, has preserved its village ambience.

*Women gather around a village well.
Most of Laos's population live in
small villages of 100–200 people.*

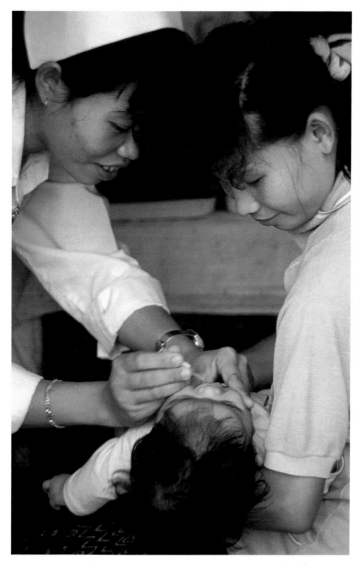

A Laotian nurse administers medication to an infant at a rural health clinic. Since 1975, the government of Laos has made significant strides in improving the nation's health care system.

Hmong children dressed in traditional clothing gather with other refugees in a camp in Thailand. Many Hmong were among the estimated 175,000 Laotians who fled their homeland when the Communist-backed Pathet Lao seized control of Laos in 1975.

Using a water buffalo to pull a plow, a Laotian family prepares the soil for planting crops. Many Laotians engage in subsistence farming, growing such crops as rice, corn, and potatoes to feed themselves.

Dressed in distinctive saffron-colored robes, young Buddhist monks, known as bonzes, walk down a street in Vientiane, the capital city of Laos. Buddhism remains an important part of life in Laos.

A boy gives his feline friend a ride in his knapsack. The children of Laos face an uncertain future as their country, one of the poorest in the world, tries to develop its economy to improve the standard of living of its citizens.

(continued from page 64)

the Indochina peninsula. By the 6th century, the worship of Buddha had extended to China, Korea, and Japan.

As with other religions, different interpretations of the sacred texts led to dispute and division, and Buddhism divided into two branches. Mahayana Buddhism, often called the Greater Vehicle, blends Buddha's teachings with Hindu beliefs to offer the hope of nirvana to all, even those who do not follow the rigorous program of the Eightfold Path. Theravada Buddhism, also known as the Lesser Vehicle or The Way of the Elders, interprets the texts more strictly, maintaining that only those who give up all earthly desire can escape suffering.

Theravada Buddhism came to Laos in about the 12th century and by the 15th century had become the primary religion of the dominant Lao Lum, though it still coexists with and is influenced by the belief in spirits. Theravada Buddhism offers some hope for the average person. Even those who have little chance of achieving nirvana in their lifetime can improve their spiritual status (karma) in their next reincarnation by avoiding the wrong things and doing the right things.

Buddhism forbids killing, stealing, lying, certain sexual practices, and strong drink or drugs. A Buddhist may earn merit and improve his or her karma through good deeds, such as showing respect to elders and performing acts of generosity. A villager may earn merit by donating money to the local *sangha* (order of Buddhist monks). For instance, one may donate money to build a *sim* (temple) or to pay for the ordination of a monk. Everyone gets a chance to earn merit at least twice a day when the bonzes (monks) file into the meeting hall of the wat. Villagers fill the bonzes' alms bowls with rice, vegetables, and delicacies. Because the donation helps the giver improve his or her karma, the donor always thanks the bonze for the chance to feed him.

Buddhist monks, called bonzes in Laos, file out of a wat, a compound of Buddhist temples and other religious structures. The wat is the central building in most Laotian villages.

The best way for a Buddhist to earn merit is to become a monk, or in the case of women, a nun. Until the Communist party assumed control, almost every Lao Lum male spent some time in the saffron-colored robe of the bonze. The monastic discipline for these novices (temporary monks) was not as stern as for the lifelong devotees. Novices must adhere to only 75 rules, whereas the full monks had to follow 227 rules. All members of the sangha shave their head, beard, and eyebrows every two weeks.

Buddhism affected many aspects of Laotian life. Until the French started a meager school system in the early 19th century, the bonzes taught Lao boys to read and write Lao and to memorize stories of Buddha in Pali, the language of the sacred texts. (Girls did not attend the sangha school.) As a state religion, Laotian Buddhism lent support to the institution of the monarchy: The king was one of the gods and therefore had a divine right to rule. The state oversaw the operation of the sangha schools and the education and ordination of the bonzes.

Since it assumed full control of the country in 1975, the Lao People's Revolutionary party (LPRP) has tolerated a variety of Buddhist activities but has also tried to reduce the independence and influence of the sanghas. By the early 1980s, some refugee monks reported that government contributions to the wats had been reduced and that many wats had started to deteriorate as donations of villagers also declined because of poor economic conditions. The government reportedly made the bonzes grow their own food, even though doing so violated their religious vows, and it banned some of the religious festivals. By 1990, however, recognizing the importance of Buddhism to Lao society, the government began to soften its opposition to Buddhism. The number of monks began to rise again, and there seems to be no overt persecution.

The Lao Tai

The Lao Tai are closely related to the Lao Lum. Their origins are the same, and their languages are so alike that speakers of Tai can understand Lao, and vice versa. Because the Lao Tai settled in remote mountain river valleys, their culture was less influenced by Indian culture. Most Lao Tai did not convert to Buddhism, for instance. They practice animism, or spirit worship.

Animists believe that all things, alive or dead, are inhabited by spirits, or *phi*. These supernatural spirits have enormous influence, for good or bad, on all human life. For example, people become ill not because of an infection but because they have angered one of the phi, and they can be cured only when the phi is appeased. Afflicted persons or their relatives will call on the local shaman, or priest, to intercede with the spirit world on their behalf. Lao Tai construct altars to the phi outside their houses. To please good spirits and ward off bad spirits, they make sacrifices of food or drink to the phi before planting, before harvest, and at every meal.

The Lao Tai, like the Lao Lum, practice terracing and wet-rice farming. They cultivate corn, wheat, and dry rice on the hillsides. They also grow cotton and flax so that they can spin and weave their own cotton and linen clothing. From silkworms raised on mulberry trees planted along the riverbanks, the Lao Tai spin lustrous silk.

Lao Tai families tend garden plots outside their village. Lao Tai live in Laos's more remote mountain river valleys and, in addition to growing their own vegetables, practice wet-rice farming.

During a festival, a Lao Tai woman wears a traditional silk skirt, known as a sin, *and a silk blouse.*

In general, the Lao Tai are much more self-sufficient than the lowland Lao, who have developed a wide trade network along the Mekong. As a result, most Lao Lum have abandoned their traditional dress in favor of Western-style clothing. In contrast, Lao Tai men still use the versatile sarong, a long piece of black-and-white-checked cotton cloth that can be wrapped around the hips as a kilt or tied between the legs to form baggy, knee-length trousers. Dipped in the water and twisted around the head in a turban, the sarong provides excellent protection from the fierce tropical sun.

Lao Tai women wear the *sin,* a panel of patterned cotton cloth that is wrapped around the body to form a calf-length skirt. For festivals and weddings, women wear silk sins with elaborately embroidered edges. Sins are worn with a long-sleeved, high-necked blouse. Some women wear straw hats in the fields; elsewhere, most wear headbands decorated with silver. Some branches of the Lao Tai— the White Tai, the Red Tai, and the Black Tai—are identified by the style and color of the blouses and headbands worn by women. Throughout rural Laos, the silver jewelry worn by the women is the family's savings account. Lao Tai and Lao Theung women tend to don headdresses, while the women of the lowland Lao wear the family's assets in the form of elaborate belts.

Instead of families and villages, Lao Tai society is organized into tribes and *muongs*. A muong is a confederacy of tribes; the word *muong* also means the district, or joint land area, of the united tribes. Before the French occupation, the chief noble, or *chao muong*, owned the entire muong. He received a certain amount of free labor on his own fields from the commoners. In many ways, the muong resembled the feudal fiefdom of medieval Europe. Below the chao muong on the political ladder were heads of smaller tribal group- ings, called *truongs*, who were also members of the nobility. The village headman, however, was always a commoner. During the protectorate, the French gave each head of a household his own land and decreed that muong leaders be elected. The conservative Lao Tai, however, simply elected their hereditary nobles to their accus- tomed positions.

The Lao Theung

The Lao Theung, who now make up about 22 percent of the popu- lation, live above the river valleys but below the 3,500-foot (1,000- meter) level. The Lao Theung are slightly smaller and have darker skin than the Lao Lum and Lao Tai. Their many dialects are part of the Mon-Khmer language family, closer to that of Cambodians than the Lao. They have no written form of their language.

The standard of living of the Lao Theung has usually been lower than that of the Lao Lum and the Lao Tai. They practice slash-and-burn agriculture, and, as a result, are seminomadic. They move their villages every few years, after all the likely fields in one location have been cleared and their soil had been exhausted. Lao Theung villages are not as self-sufficient as those of the tribal Lao. Their metalworking skills do not extend much beyond fashioning iron tips for their plows.

A blacksmith in a Lao Theung village forges a metal tool. The Lao Theung live on the mountainsides of Laos, above the river valleys but below 3,500 feet (1,000 meters).

Some Lao Theung people, like the Khmu, have long hired themselves out as wage laborers to valley farmers. Some go to Thailand to earn hard currency, in order to buy manufactured cloth, water buffalo, and other prestige items, such as metal drums and gongs. During the long civil war, both the royal government and the Pathet Lao tried to enlist the Lao Theung. The Pathet Lao recruited some Lao Theung by appealing to their resentment of the harsh treatment they had received from the lowland Lao. Most of the Pathet Lao recruits, however, were Red Tai and Khmu from the Vietnam border region. Other Lao Theung followed tradition and hired themselves out as mercenaries for the CIA-backed royal government army. The Lao Theung, who helped the Pathet Lao rise to power, have benefited most from the programs of the ruling Communist party.

The Lao Soung

The Lao Soung, who live on mountaintops throughout the country, are very different from the Lao of the valleys and the mountainsides. They are more purely Mongolian than other Lao ethnic groups, and their languages are part of the Chinese-Tibetan language family. The various tribal groups that make up the Lao Soung are fiercely independent and economically self-sufficient. Most of the Lao Soung practice animism, but they are also influenced by Chinese Buddhism and Confucianism.

The Lao Soung are the most recent arrivals in Laos. For instance, the Hmong, a prominent Lao Soung tribal group, migrated from China within the past 250 years. Other Lao Soung groups include the Man (or Yao) and the Akha. Lao Soung live above 3,500 feet (1,067 meters) and practice slash-and-burn farming, raising rice and corn as food and opium as a cash crop. The tribes are scattered throughout the highlands of Laos, Myanmar, Thailand, and southern China and do not think of themselves primarily as citizens of the particular country in which they live. The highlanders consider themselves superior to lowland dwellers, and tension exists between the various Lao Soung tribes.

A group of Lao Soung women, wearing tradition- al clothing, pause on their way to a local market. Lao Soung tribal groups — which include the Hmong, the Man, and the Akha — live on the highest moun- taintops at elevations greater than 3,500 feet (1,067 meters).

The Hmong were, until the Vietnam War, the largest and strongest group among the Lao Soung. The Laotians and French referred to them as the Meo, from *miao*, Chinese for "barbarian," but they have preserved a strong sense of pride and tradition. They live in villages of from 8 to 40 extended families, in which the sons bring

A Hmong man and his daughter enjoy a walk in Vientiane. The Hmong, who began migrating from China to Laos in the 18th century, have a strong military tradition. During the civil war, many Hmong fought for the royal government, and a large number fled Laos when Communist forces prevailed in 1975.

their wives home to live under the father's roof. The Hmong build their houses on the ground, not on stilts like the lowlanders. Each family belongs to a clan led by the oldest male. There are usually two or more clans in a village. The clan leader communicates with the clan's ancestors and the spirits. The village headman, usually the leader of the wealthiest household, has much more power than the headman of a Lao Lum village. For example, he acts as judge and assigns such community jobs as trail maintenance.

The Hmong had a strong military tradition. Customarily, in times of war the men of several associated villages elected a chieftain to lead them. His authority was absolute until his death or until the fighting men voted to depose him. This chief, or warlord, usually controlled the opium trade in his district.

To a certain extent, the Hmong have overcome Lao prejudice against highlanders. Aggressive and well-disciplined, they have always refused to be pushed around. The cash from the opium trade has insulated them to some extent from crop failure. They were the only tribal people with elected representatives in the pre-1975 legislature.

During the civil war, most Hmong sided with the royal government, although one branch, the White Hmong, fought alongside Pathet Lao rebels. Year after year, Hmong warriors, whose warlords were paid and directed by the CIA, kept Pathet Lao guerrillas and Vietnamese regular troops from sweeping across the Plain of Jars and taking control of the country.

The cost of war was high to the Hmong. More than 10,000 died in action between 1960 and 1970; countless more, including women and children, died in bombing raids and in the wholesale defeat that followed the U.S. withdrawal. After the Communist takeover, thousands of Hmong fled the country. Although some were airlifted to the United States, most remain in refugee camps in Thailand.

The Man (called the Yao in China), like the Hmong, live at high altitudes. The Man have a very high regard for money. Wealthy tribesmen endeavor to ensure high rank in the afterlife by paying silver to the spirits in a series of rites. One pays more, of course, as one climbs the spiritual ladder. The title used by a living tribesman indicates which rituals he has paid for so far. The Man do not have the strong ties among villages that the Hmong do. They have a reputation as peacemakers, willing to go to great lengths to avoid conflict.

The languages of other Lao Soung tribal groups suggest that their ancestors came from Tibet. Of these groups, most of whom live in Myanmar and Thailand, the Akha are the most numerous in Laos. Like the Man, the Akha have little or no concern with life outside their village. They are elusive, preferring to move farther into the wilderness when faced with any challenge from the outside world.

Using log stilts and woven bamboo slats, two men construct a house in a small Laotian village. Most houses in Laos are built on stilts to raise them above the floods and swampy conditions caused by monsoon rains.

6

Village Life

Most of the people of Laos live in small rural settlements near a stream or river. A typical Lao Lum village is situated on a tributary of the Mekong. Above the village, the green wall of the rain forest is broken where a smaller stream snakes its way down from the hills. The level stretch between stream and river is crisscrossed by black dikes; behind the dikes, green rice seedlings rise from patches of water.

Along the bank, tall coconut palms lean over the river. A rickety dock floats on bamboo poles. Tied to the dock are a dugout pirogue and a larger boat with a thatched roof and a pair of upright poles bristling from both stern and bow: This is a sampan, a fishing boat. Fishermen string nets between the poles and lower them into the river to scoop up mullet and perch.

A row of bushy mulberry trees marks the course of the canal that brings upstream water to the paddies. Beyond the paddies on the slope above flood level are the houses. Rectangular, with walls of woven bamboo poles and thatched roofs, they sit 6 to 8 feet (1.8 to 2.4 meters) above the ground on sturdy log pilings.

Housing

The houses in a typical village are spaced at least 60 to 70 feet (20 to 22 meters) apart. Depending upon the size and wealth of the household, a house is 20 to 40 feet (6 to 12 meters) in length. An inclined ladder or a set of unrailed steps leads to the veranda, a roofed porch that runs across the front of the single floor of the house. In most houses, bamboo screens roll down from the roof to keep out rain. The veranda serves as the common room of the house, a combination living room, kitchen, and dining room.

Behind the veranda, a partition runs the length of the house, dividing it into a large front room and a row of smaller rooms, each with its own door into the front room. The front room has a hearth and a family altar dedicated to the phi. Like the veranda, it is part of the household's public space. The back rooms, one for each family member, are for sleeping. Unmarried young men usually sleep on the veranda or in the front room. Furniture is simple and scarce—a modest table, a few chairs, and shelves and baskets for storing clothes and other belongings. Everyone sleeps on mats on the floor.

Wooden planks form the floors of the house. The interior walls of woven bamboo do not reach the roof, and this helps air circulate more freely. Windows are small, making the interiors rather dark and stuffy. More prosperous villagers build their houses with wooden plank walls and corrugated tin roofs, which makes them more weatherproof but darker and stuffier than those with bamboo walls. A larger village might even boast a brick building or two.

The Household

The typical household in Laos consists of a mother and father, their children, and dependent relatives, such as unmarried sisters and grandparents. Married sons bring their brides to stay under their family's roof until they are able to begin their own households, which usually means until they have children of their own who are

A man enjoys his dinner, which includes rice, the staple food of the Laotian diet. Laotian food is a mixture of hot and sweet tastes.

old enough to work in the house and fields. In small, remote villages, each household produces virtually everything that it consumes, including food, clothing, tools, fishing gear, and boats. What little cash the family has is used to buy iron products, kerosene for lamps and stoves, and salt.

Usually, each house has its own garden and fruit trees. In addition to bananas, Lao villagers grow mangoes, avocados, grapefruits, lemons, limes, litchis, and pears. Gardens contain cucumbers, salad greens, cassava (an edible root), yams, eggplants, onions, and several kinds of chili peppers, which play an important role in the diet. Laotian food, similar to the food of Thailand, is a mixture of hot and sweet tastes. Curry dishes are popular, and in many recipes the fiery bite of peppers is balanced by the soothing sweetness of coconut milk. The mainstay of the village diet is sticky rice, which family members eat from a communal bowl. They use their fingers to roll the rice into balls and then dip the balls into various sauces. A favorite sauce is *nam pa*, a thick paste made by filtering water through salted and dried fish. Nam pa, eggs, fresh fish, and chicken are important sources of protein.

Most of rural Laos has no indoor plumbing or electricity. In some villages, each house has its own outhouse, which sometimes has a septic tank. Elsewhere, people dig a shallow hole to defecate, then cover it with soil. In spite of such austere conditions, the Lao are

A young child tends the family water buffalo. Most village families must be self-suffi-cient, which requires all family members—including the young and the elderly—to con-tribute by working in the fields or performing household chores.

By using a traditional wooden mortar and pestle to pound rice, village women separate the rice kernels from their hulls.

very cleanly people. They wash before and after meals and bathe daily in the river.

Cleanliness, however, is no sure guard against disease because unsanitary water harbors bacteria that can cause dysentery, typhoid, and cholera. The French colonial government and the royal government fairly successfully controlled cholera through inoculation programs, at least in the towns and larger villages.

During the 1970s, however, dysentery was one of the major causes of death in Laos. Malaria, a tropical disease transmitted among humans by the bites of infected mosquitoes, remains a major health hazard.

Most village houses have sheds for animals and a granary to store rice. Often, the family water buffalo, an enduring symbol of rural Asia, is tethered to a betel tree in the yard. Farmers use buffalo to plow the thick mud of the paddies, to drag soil and earth into paddy dikes, and to pull wagons. Unlike their fierce wild cousins, water buffalo are patient, gentle beasts, and their upkeep is usually assigned to younger children, who can easily lead them around and safely climb on their broad backs.

The division of labor among the family is based on gender and age. Men plow the fields and perform other heavy work. They fish, hunt, and build canoes and wagons. Whenever possible, men work in the forest, logging or collecting forest products to sell to traders. Women cook, clean, spin and weave, and maintain the gardens. Women's work is difficult. Preparing a meal, for example, requires carrying water from the river or village well; carrying wood to houses without kerosene stoves; hulling the rice by pounding it in the heavy, foot-driven mortar and pestle; picking, cleaning, and preparing garden produce; and, on special occasions, catching and killing a chicken. Women also do the marketing—both buying necessities and selling surpluses.

In a subsistence economy, one in which families are only able to produce enough for themselves with little surplus, the contributions of old and young are vital. While the mothers are working in the garden or planting seedlings in the rice paddies, grandmothers care for young children and prepare meals. Older children help with the household chores, tend the animals, and work in the garden. Old people who are too feeble for even the lightest chores retain the respect and affection of the household. Many older men devote their days to meditation and prayer.

Religion and the Village

The most impressive structure in most villages is the wat. Every Lao Lum village has a wat; larger villages and towns have several. A wat consists of several Buddhist temples and other buildings surrounded by a whitewashed fence with elaborate gates. The temples are made of brick and have steep roofs of red tile. Each wat also contains a large wooden meeting hall and bungalows housing the members of the Buddhist monastery.

Before the change in government in 1975, the wat was the center of village life. At noon each day, the bonzes filed into the wat meeting hall to the boom of a buffalo-hide drum. The women of the village brought pots of food, which they ladled into the bowls of the kneeling monks. Besides the daily donations, villagers came to the wat several times a week to observe holy days and special ceremonies. Boys between 10 and 15 years old came to the wat every day to perform housecleaning chores, to assist at rites, and to be instructed in reading, writing, and memorizing stories of Buddha.

The wat remains the site of the many religious festivals and fairs (called *bouns*) that dot the Laotian calendar. Festivals, such as the long New Year celebration, are important to the religious, economic, and social life of everyone in the village. For the Lao, the year begins at the end of the dry season, usually around April. The bonzes determine the exact date each year according to astrological signs. A procession of floats, masked marchers, and holy images ushers out the old year. The people sweep out their houses, in order to rid them of any bad spirits that may have sneaked in during the year. On the first day of the new year, the shaven-headed monks in their saffron-colored robes lead a procession to the sim, or temple. There they cleanse the images of Buddha by sprinkling them with holy water. Villagers build prayer mounds of sand or stone in the courtyard of the temple and along the banks of the river. Tiny prayer flags fly from the top of the mounds.

Dressed in their finest clothes, people visit each other's houses, which are decorated with colorful paper streamers bearing the signs of the zodiac. In the evening, everyone gathers in the open space before the wat, where electric lights or kerosene lanterns hang in the trees.

Under the palm trees, men squat on their haunches to play the complicated card game called *phay tong* or to watch and bet on a board game similar to checkers. The men leave the gambling circles to buy glasses of *satho*, sweet rice wine. The Buddhist prohibition against intoxicating drink is relaxed at festival time. Satho is pretty mild stuff, and the Lao Lum rarely overdo it.

On a stage at one end of the courtyard, a traveling troupe of dancers perform a ballet version of a story from the Indian epic *Ramayana*. At other festivals, the villagers themselves put on traditional dances, complete with elaborate costumes and masks, to dramatize a historic event or to placate the spirit world. Another popular entertainment is the shadow play, in which the silhouettes of puppets are thrown onto a screen between performers and audience.

Musicians who travel from festival to festival supply the music. The most popular instrument is the *khene*, a reed pipe made of five or so bamboo tubes tied together, each cut to variant lengths to produce different notes. The *nang-nat* is a xylophonelike arrangement of bamboo tubes, and the *so* is a string instrument played with a bow, like a violin. Flutes, drums, cymbals, and tambourines add to the band.

Later, village girls and boys dance the *lamvong*, a combination folk dance and courting ritual. Girls dance in place with short, rhythmic steps, while boys weave circles around them; no one touches. The faces of the dancers are intent and completely expressionless, but their arms and hands wave in complicated patterns expressive of love and devotion.

During a festival, a musician blows on a reed pipe known as a khene. *Other traditional Laotian instruments include the* nang-nat, *which is similar to a xylophone, and the* so, *a stringed instrument played with a bow.*

Laotians are much more boisterous during Bang-Fay, the triple festival marking the birth, enlightenment, and death of Buddha. Bang-Fay falls at the full moon in May, the time of planting in Laos. Many of the events of the festival are connected with fertility rites practiced long before the arrival of Buddhism. During Bang-Fay, tipsy young men parade through the village beating on drums and oilcans and singing bawdy songs. Some carry male and female marionettes, called *zobristes*, that they manipulate to mimic sexual intercourse, thus encouraging, by example, the earth to be fruitful.

Bang-Fay is also the time for tremendous fireworks shows. Competing groups fashion 30-foot (9-meter) tubes of bamboo and paper and paint them to represent sacred dragons. The slender tubes are decorated with streamers and flowers and packed full of gunpowder. To the sound of drums and cymbals, young men dance their colorful rockets through the village to rickety bamboo scaffolds on the riverbank. From a platform, they set off the rockets, which explode in a bright shower above the river.

The noise of the fireworks is believed to cause the skies to open up and pour down the long-awaited rain. According to an ancient legend, the guests at the wedding of a Lao princess set the heavens on fire with their fireworks. The inhabitants of heaven called for help to the Hindu god Indra, and he put out the fire with the monsoon.

Khao Vatsa is a quieter festival. It occurs during the full moon of July, just at the height of the rainy season. It marks the beginning of a three-month-long retreat for the bonzes. During this period, the bonzes increase their devotions and meditations and limit their contact with the villagers. Any village man who chooses this period to serve as a novice monk earns extra merit. During the festival called Ho Khao Slak, which falls around the end of September, villagers, who are selected by lot, have the privilege of donating gifts to the bonzes, who remain confined to the wat. Boun Ok Vassa, at the end of the rainy season, celebrates the end of the bonzes' retreat. It is the time for the more devout Buddhists to set out on pilgrimages to holy places within Laos and as far away as India. Villagers outfit bonzes with new robes, sleeping mats, and begging bowls. The climax of the festival is a series of pirogue races. These and other festivals mark the seasons of the year and keep the cycle of village life turning.

The Life Cycle

The first big event for a Lao is the naming ceremony. The family hosts a feast, or *baci*, in its house for the rest of the village. The size of the feast depends upon the wealth of the family. A bonze usually chooses a name according to the prevailing astrological conditions. The given name might be that of a flower, tree, or color. Family members will probably call the child by a nickname. Until the government made family names mandatory shortly after World War II, Laotians did not always use them; children did not automatically have the same last name as the father. Even today, Laotians are fairly relaxed and inventive about names. A Laotian man might change his name several times during his life, to mark changes in career or status or to fool evil spirits.

Children in rural villages learn the skills of village life from parents, grandparents, and older brothers and sisters. Before the new government took power and established public schools

During a baci—*a feast highlighted by a ceremony in which a newborn is given his or her name— a mother holds her child while rolls of money are tied to the infant's arm.*

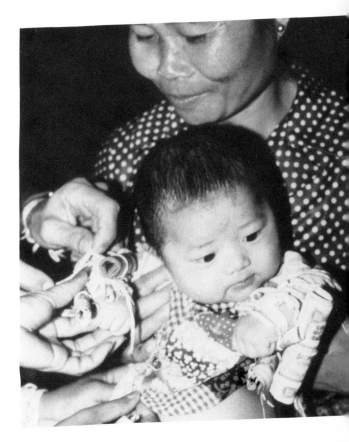

throughout the country, one boy from each family would have attended school at the wat between the ages of 10 and 13. He would have learned to read and write Lao; boys destined to become bonzes would have learned Pali, the ancient Hindu language of the Buddhist scriptures. Traditionally, only boys went to school, and then only when they were not needed in the fields or for fishing and forest work.

The next important ceremony in a Lao boy's life marks his transition from childhood to adulthood, around the age of 13. Only the immediate family and close relatives attend the ritual, which includes cutting the boy's hair. In more traditional villages, the boy might still receive a tattoo, which is considered an essential mark of manhood and is believed to ward off evil spirits.

Between the manhood ceremony and marriage, most Lao boys formerly entered the sangha for a brief period as a monk, to gain merit both for themselves and their family. This was considered an important event in a boy's spiritual life, to be celebrated with a feast for the village, if the family could afford it. This tradition has diminished in present-day Laos.

Laotian men usually marry when in their twenties. The bride is usually younger, still in her teens. She will most likely be from the same village and will probably be related in some degree because most villages are small. Couples choose each other, but the heads of both families decide when the couple will marry, where they will live, and what bride-price must be paid to the girl's father. This is usually in currency, although in olden times it was in livestock or grain.

The groom's family delivers the bride-price to the bride's father on the day before the wedding. The groom's relatives parade to the bride's house with gifts of food, tobacco, betel, and so on. The groom makes his formal request for the bride; her family, after a long-winded, purely ceremonial show of reluctance, finally agrees. In the presence of a bonze or village elder, the couple are officially betrothed. The next day, the groom and his relatives again proceed to the bride's house, where they make a great show of fighting and bribing their way into the yard. The groom must persuade the bride's sister to wash his feet before he can ascend the steps to the house and claim his bride.

Divorce is rare in Laos, partly because each marriage concerns everyone in two large, extended families. If a marriage is dissolved, the bride-price has to be returned, and there are endless complications concerning inheritance and land use. It is much more sensible to compromise. Working things out is, in general, the Laotian response to almost every conflict.

The funeral is the last and possibly the most important ceremony for a Laotian. Bonzes are more intimately involved in funerals than in baptism, marriage, or childbirth. They pray for the spirit's swift passage to a new incarnation and recite the Pali hymns that tell of the necessity of death for the soul's rebirth.

The family prepares the body for cremation and arranges it in a coffin in the yard of the house, where a series of ceremonies and feasts begin. Each group to which the deceased belonged in life says good-bye. Relatives on both the mother's and the father's side; brothers and sisters and their families; the children and their families; co-workers, friends, and acquaintances—all troop through, sharing food, drink, and memories. The mood is upbeat; to act sad implies that you do not think much of the departed's chances in the next turn of the wheel of life.

The period of prayers and feasts lasts for two to three days, even longer for wealthier families. Then the coffin is carried to the pyre, a pile of burning logs on the riverbank. There, the family opens the coffin to wash the body and expose it to the sky. Everyone throws a piece of burning wood on the body and watches as the flames consume coffin, corpse, and pyre. Then the feasting begins again, along with wrestling matches, cockfights, and discussions of the virtues of the deceased.

In the center of Vientiane, an honor guard stands watch at a military memorial commemorating those killed in action during Laos's civil war. When it assumed control of the government in 1975, the Lao People's Revolutionary party immediately began rebuilding the war-torn and undeveloped country.

7

Laos Today and Tomorrow

By the end of the Second Indochina War in 1975, Laos hardly existed as a country. For 300 years before its independence in 1949, Laos had been divided into petty states that were ruled by outsiders most of the time. Laos had no history of self-government, and the few schools established by the French did not prepare Laotians to run their country. Most Laotians were illiterate farmers with no sense of allegiance to anything as abstract as a nation. Laos had almost no middle class, and the ruling class consisted of the members of about 200 interrelated families who had little in common with the mass of the people. To receive any education higher than the grade school level, Laotians had to go to France or Vietnam. In short, Laos lacked a social infrastructure: It did not have the social systems, such as schools and a civil service, that support a nation.

The nation's physical structures were also inadequate. When the French left, there were few paved roads, no railroads, and few municipal water, sewer, and electric systems. The United Nations and many developed countries poured millions of dollars in aid into Laos after it gained independence. Most of the funds were used in much-needed public health programs, well-digging projects, and road building. By 1975, however, after 20 years of civil war, most of the roads, as well as much of the country, were in ruins. Laos had a great deal to rebuild. Since then, according to reports by such organizations as the World Bank and the United Nations relief agencies, the country has come a long way.

Health

Public health care has improved, particularly in the cities. With assistance from the Soviet Union, the Laotian government built a major hospital in Vientiane. There is still much to be done. Laos has only 1 doctor for every 3,500 people, and 1 hospital bed for every 400 people. The infant mortality rate of about 97 deaths per 1,000 live births is among the highest in the world. Life expectancy at birth is only 51 years for men and 54 years for women. Malnutrition causes serious health problems, especially for children. Many Laotians still go to bed hungry each night.

Education

Upon assuming control of the country, the Lao People's Revolutionary party (LPRP) announced its goal of providing a basic education for every child and teaching all adults to read. Primary education now begins at six years of age. Secondary education, beginning at age 11, lasts for 6 years. By 1986, there were more than 7,000 schools in which more than half of the school-age population was enrolled. Most Laotians desire a better education, and the literacy rate has increased dramatically since 1975.

The government appears sincere in its commitment to increase educational opportunity. Laos has greatly expanded its vocational training system, now operating dozens of schools attended by more than 21,000 trainees annually. For example, the Lao German Technical School, established in the 1960s with West German assistance, instructs about 200 people each year in electronics and mechanics. In addition, the government has established medical and teacher-training colleges in Vientiane, Luang Prabang, and Savannakhet to prepare the doctors and teachers that the nation

Primary school children study in a school in the village of Nong Khoey. Laos has greatly expanded its educational system since 1975.

desperately needs. The country's one university is in Vientiane. Education has improved, but many Laotians still must go outside the country, especially to Vietnam or even as far as Europe, for higher education.

Economy

In spite of assistance from other nations and international agencies, Laos is one of the world's most underdeveloped countries. Because it has few factories, only about 17 percent of its gross domestic product (GDP) comes from industry. The GDP is the value of all goods and services that a country produces in one year. Though Laos's GDP has grown rapidly in recent years, it is estimated at only $850 to $1,100 per capita in U.S. dollars.

Most of the GDP comes from the export of hydroelectric power, timber, and tin. Laos has significant deposits of other raw materials, such as coal and iron ore and other metals, and forests cover approximately half of the country. However, because of rugged terrain, poor roads, and the lack of capital, it will be a long time before Laos can exploit those resources.

Approximately 80 percent of the labor force is still devoted to agriculture. Despite the rich soil of the Mekong Valley, Laos often must import food, in part because of the lack of transportation. Because they cannot get their goods to market, villages do not usually raise any surplus. Crops are heavily dependent upon weather conditions, particularly floods and droughts. Rice shortages still occur periodically.

At present, Laos must import much more than it can export, although the gap has narrowed in recent years. Generally the infrastructure needed for economic progress is still lacking. By some estimates, there are only about 9,000 miles (15,000 km) of highways in the country, and less than 20 percent of them are paved. Because much of the land is mountainous and there is a long rainy season, dirt roads are often nearly impassable. Railroads are nonexistent, and the scheduled flights of the airline, Lao Aviation, are limited. The Mekong remains the main transportation artery. When the Friendship Bridge, a span across the Mekong near Vientiane, opened in 1994 to link Laos with Thailand, the ceremony was a major event. It featured the Laotian prime minister, the king and prime minister of Thailand, and the prime minister of Australia, whose government had funded the project. Yet some people worried that this connection would give Thai entrepreneurs a better chance to exploit Laotian natural resources without necessarily benefiting Laos.

The Future

Threats to the political stability of Southeast Asia persist. Border disputes between Laos and Thailand and between Laos and Myanmar flare up sporadically. Warlords rule the opium-rich region called the Golden Triangle where Laos, Myanmar, and

These rows of electronic goods in a Vientiane store form a stark contrast to the lack of modern services in most of the countryside.

Thailand meet. Political violence among rival factions has continued in Cambodia. Chinese animosity toward Vietnam still smolders. As in the past, any widespread eruption of conflict among its neighbors would probably involve Laos. On the whole, however, prospects for peace and development in Southeast Asia appear as bright as they have been in a generation.

Change will come to Laos. There are roads to be built and sanitation, clean water, and electricity to be brought to the towns and the countryside. Laos must improve its agriculture, build a manufacturing base, and sell enough of its products to improve the material well-being of its people. In order for these things to happen, the ancient rhythms of life on the Mekong must be changed, and new patterns of living must be adopted. Perhaps Laos can achieve these goals without losing the wealth of its culture or undermining the spirit of its people.

GLOSSARY

animism   The belief that a spirit or force resides in every object and living thing.

betel   A large palm tree whose seed, the betel nut, is chewed for its mild narcotic effect.

bonze   A Buddhist monk.

colugo   A lemur capable of gliding on webs of membrane stretched between its neck and forelegs, between its legs, and between its rear legs and tail.

cordillera   A system of mountain ranges forming a more or less continuous chain.

floodplain   Level land that is periodically flooded; a plain made up of silt deposited by the receding floodwaters of a river.

gaur   Wild ox found in the forests of Southeast Asia.

gibbon   A small ape native to the forests of Southeast Asia.

junk   A ship of traditional Chinese design with steep sides, high decks at bow and stern, and one or more pole masts; present- day junks have diesel-driven propellers as well.

karst   Terrain formed by limestone deposits and marked by sharp ridges, steep, conical hills, sinks, and underground rivers.

laterization   A process by which moist, warm climatic conditions cause tropical soil to lose nutrients; laterite soil is red.

khene   Musical instrument; reed pipe of five to seven bamboo tubes of various lengths.

landlocked   Enclosed by land; a landlocked country does not border or have a port on an ocean or sea.

muong   A grouping of Lao Tai tribes; the muong is also the province or district made up of the land owned by the tribes.

Pali   The ancient Indian language used in the sacred writings of Theravada Buddhism.

phi   A spirit or spirits; in the animist belief of the Lao Tai, phi exist in every living and inanimate thing and influence everything that happens.

pirogue   A canoe used in China and Southeast Asia; traditionally pirogues were dugouts, formed from tree trunks.

sampan   A flat-bottomed boat, powered by oars or a diesel-driven propeller.

sangha   An order of Buddhist monks.

sim   A Buddhist temple.

that   A stupa, a stone mound or tower built to hold a Buddhist relic.

wat   A Buddhist temple compound.

INDEX

Souvanna Phouma, prince of
  Laos, 55, 56
Soviet Union, 18, 100

T

Temples. *See* Buddhist shrines
Thailand, 17, 22, 25, 26, 27, 28, 29,
  41, 45, 47, 49, 51–52, 53, 58, 62,
  80, 83, 102
Thakhek, 29
That (stone tower), 29
That Luang shrine, 19, 29, 44, 47
Theravada Buddhism, 63, 73
Tran Ninh Plateau, 31–33
Transportation, 22, 31, 99, 102
Truongs, 78

U

United Nations, 29, 99, 100
United States, 18, 29, 55, 56–57,
  59, 83, 103

V

Van Wuysthoff, Gerrit, 48
Vientiane, 19, 20, 24, 28–29, 57,
  100, 101
Vientiane, kingdom of, 49
Vietcong, 56
Vietminh, 53, 54, 55
Vietnam, 17, 18, 19, 21, 22, 31, 45,
  47, 48, 51, 52, 54, 55, 58, 101
Vietnam War, 55–57

W

Wat (temple compound), 29, 45,
  46, 47, 74, 91
Wat Pra Keo, 29, 47
World War II, 17, 33, 53

X

Xieng Khouang, 48, 49

Y

Yao. *See* Man

PICTURE CREDITS